The *Titanic* Tragedy

PERSPECTIVES ON

The *Titanic* Tragedy
The Price of Prosperity in a Gilded Age

JEFF BURLINGAME

Marshall Cavendish
Benchmark
New York

Published by Marshall Cavendish Benchmark
An imprint of Marshall Cavendish Corporation

This publication represents the opinions and views of the author based on Jeff Burlingame's personal
experience, knowledge, and research. The information in this book serves as a general guide only. The
author and publisher have used their best efforts in preparing this book and disclaim liability rising
directly and indirectly from the use and application of this book.

Other Marshall Cavendish Offices:
Marshall Cavendish International (Asia) Private Limited, 1 New Industrial Road, Singapore 536196
• Marshall Cavendish International (Thailand) Co Ltd. 253 Asoke, 12th Flr, Sukhumvit 21 Road,
Klongtoey Nua, Wattana, Bangkok 10110, Thailand • Marshall Cavendish (Malaysia) Sdn Bhd,
Times Subang, Lot 46, Subang Hi-Tech Industrial Park, Batu Tiga, 40000 Shah Alam, Selangor Darul
Ehsan, Malaysia

Marshall Cavendish is a trademark of Times Publishing Limited

All websites were available and accurate when this book was sent to press.

Library of Congress Cataloging-in-Publication Data
Burlingame, Jeff.
The Titanic tragedy / Jeff Burlingame.
p. cm. — (Perspectives on)
Includes bibliographical references and index.
Summary: "Provides comprehensive information on the Titanic tragedy and the differing perspectives
accompanying it"—Provided by publisher.
ISBN 978-1-60870-450-7 (print) ISBN 978-1-60870-722-5 (ebook)
1. Titanic (Steamship)—Juvenile literature. 2. Shipwrecks—North Atlantic Ocean—Juvenile
literature. I. Title.
G530.T6B86 2012
910.9163'4—dc22
2010041560

Editor: Christine Florie
Publisher: Michelle Bisson
Art Director: Anahid Hamparian
Series Designer: Sonia Chaghatzbanian

Expert Reader: Karen Kamuda, Titanic Historical Society, Indian Orchard, Massachusetts

Photo research by Marybeth Kavanagh

Cover photo by Getty Images

The photographs in this book are used by permission and through the courtesy of: *The Bridgeman Art
Library*: Look and Learn, 2-3; *Alamy*: World History Archive, 8; Mary Evans Picture Library, 19, 31;
INTERFOTO, 20; Everett Collection Inc., 52; Pictorial Press Ltd., 66; *North Wind Picture Archives*: 11;
SuperStock: Science and Society, 15; Image Asset Management Ltd., 21, 38, 40, 54; Everett Collection,
79; *Getty Images*: Hulton Archive, 16; *akg-images*: Universal Images Group, 23, 24, 25, 48, 87, 91; *The
Image Works*: Topham, 29; The Print Collector/HIP, 62; *Corbis*: Bettmann, 30; *Newscom*: akg-images, 35,
45; Daily Mirror, 50; Timothy A. Clary/AFP/Getty Images, 83; Matthew Tulloch, 84; *AP Photo*: Bullit
Marquez, 76; Bob Child, 80

Printed in Printed in Malaysia (T)
135642

Contents

Introduction

INITIAL REPORTS WERE SKETCHY and often wildly inaccurate. That the much-touted ocean liner Royal Mail Ship, or RMS, *Titanic* had struck an iceberg in the North Atlantic Ocean was the only consistent piece of information. Within a day or so the basic facts were determined, and when they were reported, the world reacted with shock and sorrow. An iceberg lying off the coast of Newfoundland, Canada, weighing approximately 250,000 tons, had been in the *Titanic's* path. The vessel collided with the obstacle in the late evening hours of April 14, 1912, and thousands of gallons of frigid seawater rapidly filled the hull until the ship could take no more. At 2:20 a.m. on April 15, the *Titanic* sank to the bottom of the ocean. More than 1,500 people—rich and poor; men, women, and children—were killed. It was the deadliest accident in maritime history at that time.

How could such a tragedy take place on a state-of-the-art ship that had been declared "unsinkable"? The world wanted answers and someone or something at which to point the angry finger of blame. Certainly the victims' families, grieving in more than twenty countries, needed a thorough explanation. So did the general public and politicians.

Was the *Titanic's* captain at fault for failing to reduce the ship's speed as it traveled through an area known to have icebergs? Was the great loss of life due to the failure of the ship's owner to provide enough lifeboats to seat all of the more than 2,200 people on board? Was the *Titanic's* captain to blame for not making sure that all the seats were filled on the lifeboats that were available? Or was the captain of the nearby British freighter *Californian* to blame for failing to recognize and respond to the many rocket flares originating from the sinking *Titanic*? Was the disaster the result of these factors combined, or something else entirely?

The wreck of the *Titanic* occurred during America's Gilded Age, a period following the U.S. Civil War (1861–1865) that saw the rise of powerful corporations. While the businessmen who owned these corporations became enormously wealthy, many of those who provided labor lived in extreme poverty. The privileged class of the Gilded Age flaunted its wealth in many ways. Travel was one of them, and the *Titanic* had been created with this clientele in mind. Its purpose was to dominate the North Atlantic luxury travel market by offering an opulent experience the likes of which had never been seen. Were safety and the lives of 1,500 innocent people sacrificed to achieve this goal?

The lessons learned from the disaster continue to impact the way the shipping industry is regulated. With each large-scale maritime tragedy since, new rules have been created. But even some one hundred years after the *Titanic's* sinking, the importance of learning from history's best-known maritime disaster has not diminished. Only by analyzing the stories of those involved in the *Titanic* tragedy can we expect to avoid repeating the mistakes that led to the legendary disaster.

One

An "Unsinkable" Ship

VIOLET JESSOP WAS ALMOST ASLEEP in her bunk in the crew quarters of the *Titanic* when the crash jarred her awake, shortly before midnight on April 14, 1912. The sound of crunching and ripping metal that followed filled the young stewardess with fear, and hearing the mighty ship's engines shut down did nothing to assuage it. Outside the cabin door she heard workers rushing to duty. The quiet, star-filled night on the North Atlantic—the fourth day of what was to be a weeklong voyage—was quiet no longer. The mighty *Titanic* had struck an iceberg and was taking on water. In the memoirs she wrote nearly a quarter-century later, Jessop recalled the dread she felt the moment a fellow steward told her the news: their unsinkable workplace was going down.

> Sinking? Of course *Titanic* couldn't be
> sinking! What nonsense! She so perfect, so
> new—yet now she was so still, so inanimate;
> not a sound after that awful grinding crash.
> She that had so short a time ago been so
> vital was now the embodiment of immobility.

The grand luxury liner *Titanic* struck an iceberg and sank in the North Atlantic Ocean.

> My mind, usually adjustable to sudden and
> unforeseen happenings, could not accept the
> fact that this superperfect creation was to do
> so futile a thing as sink.

Of course, Jessop could not know what was to follow,
nor could she imagine the great impact the event she was
now a part of would have on the world for decades to come.
As she helped passengers fasten their lifebelts, she had no
idea that in less than three hours the massive ship she had
worked and lived on for four days would be under water,
or that more than 1,500 people would go down with or near
it. Jessop did not know that she would be one of the lucky
ones—she would have a seat in one of the too-few lifeboats.
Carrying a passenger's baby in her arms, she would be
bounced around in the ocean for hours before being rescued
by the British passenger steamship *Carpathia*.

Battle for Sea Supremacy

The *Titanic*—and its two sister ships, the *Olympic* and the
Britannic—had been conceived by the White Star Line. The
ships were the company's response to the battle for market
supremacy in transporting wealthy businessmen and their
families, middle-class vacationers, immigrants, and others
across the Atlantic Ocean between America and Europe.

The genesis of that battle had come decades earlier, following the Civil War. At that time, the United States had
entered a period of economic expansion during which the
wealth of many Americans significantly grew, thanks in
part to the country's westward expansion and to new tech-
nologies that strengthened industry and trade. The Gilded

Age—alternately known at various times in England as the Victorian Age and the Edwardian Age—lasted roughly from the mid–1860s until the early 1900s. During this time, the wealth gap between America's rich and poor reached unprecedented proportions. The era coincided with a population boom brought about by the arrival of hundreds of thousands of immigrants, who had come to the United States in search of a better life. Few found it. Most were relegated to low-paying jobs or went without work, which left them in poverty, fighting to stay alive in substandard

The Gilded Age was an era of economic growth, during which some achieved great wealth.

tenement housing that was springing up in the larger cities. Meanwhile, rich entrepreneurs such as Andrew Carnegie, John D. Rockefeller, and Cornelius Vanderbilt lived the lavish lifestyles that came to exemplify the Gilded Age.

Traveling was a favorite pastime for the privileged few during America's Gilded Age. Those who wished to visit European cities frequently arrived on the Continent after having crossed the North Atlantic in extravagantly luxurious steam yachts. Many such voyages were highly publicized. The transatlantic trips of shipping and railroad tycoon Vanderbilt aboard his *North Star*, for example, were deemed significant enough to warrant coverage in *The New York Times*. Soon, the countries to which wealthy Americans were traveling—chiefly Germany, England, and France—began a battle to corner the market on those who could afford regular journeys across the North Atlantic. To gain market share, shipping lines focused not only on building the biggest, most luxurious ships but also on making them capable of crossing the ocean as quickly as possible. An unofficial award called the Blue Riband, or Blue Ribbon, was created and given to the passenger ship that made the trip with the fastest average speed, and competition for the title was fierce. The shipping company that held the title gained both prestige and profits.

Saving the White Star Line

England's Cunard Line began its domination of the North Atlantic market in the early 1840s and continued to surpass the other shipping companies for decades, capturing several Blue Riband awards along the way. A challenge to Cunard's long-term dominance began to take shape in 1867,

The Gilded Age

The term "Gilded Age" was derived from the novel *The Gilded Age: A Tale of To-day*, written in 1873 by Mark Twain and Charles Dudley Warner. The fictional book was a satirical exposé of the greed and political corruption the authors believed was rampant throughout the United States at the time, *gilded* being a word that describes something made to look pretty on the outside to cover up ugliness that exists inside. The term became widely used, and still is used today to represent a period in history defined by its extravagance and exploitation.

History of the Blue Riband

Originally awarded in 1838 by transatlantic shipping companies, the Blue Riband was for nearly a century the benchmark for crossings of the Atlantic Ocean by ocean liners. To win the title, a ship had to have the fastest average speed in nautical miles per hour (knots) between the Bishop Rock lightship (moored in the Isles of Scilly just off Cornwall, England) and the Ambrose lightship at the mouth of New York Harbor. The last winner was the SS *United States* in 1952, which completed the voyage with an average speed of 35.6 knots.

Thomas Henry Ismay, the son of a shipbuilder, bought the White Star Line. At the time of Ismay's death, it was the most profitable company in the world.

when a forward-thinking thirty-year-old Englishman named Thomas Ismay purchased the nearly bankrupt White Star Line. Ismay, the son of a boat builder, had a grand vision for his newly acquired company. Prior to Ismay's takeover, the White Star fleet consisted of wooden ships whose primary mission was transporting gold seekers from England to Australia. Ismay proceeded to refocus the company: in 1869 he created the Oceanic Steam Navigation Company; then he partnered with shipbuilders Harland and Wolff of Belfast to create a new fleet of iron steamships. His goal was to capture the North Atlantic passenger market.

The first ship Harland and Wolff built for the White Star Line was the *Oceanic I*. It was the first vessel to have promenade decks, bathtubs with hot and cold running water, oil lamps, and steam heat for its passengers. Separate accommodations were offered to first-class passengers, whose cabins, located in the ship's calmer midsection, were larger than any cabins ever had been. Meanwhile, lower-class passengers

White Star's first ocean liner was the RMS *Oceanic*, which launched in 1870. It was one of the finest vessels of its day.

were housed in the front and rear sections of the ship. The *Oceanic* was hailed at the time as being "more like an imperial yacht than a passenger liner." In 1871 the 420-foot-long *Oceanic* made its maiden voyage across the North Atlantic from Liverpool to New York. Within a few years, the *Oceanic* was joined by three identical sister ships (*Atlantic*, *Baltic*, and *Republic*) and two slightly larger ones (*Adriatic* and *Celtic*). They were all built by Harland and Wolff and commissioned by White Star under the direction of Ismay, who eventually became known as the man who paved the way for modern luxury ships. Sir Bertram Hayes, who in 1891 would become the captain of a White Star Line ship, said Ismay had helped break new ground in the industry.

I consider that he was the most far seeing
man of steamers, and I am not sure that
the travelling public have ever realized the
debt they owe to his foresight. He was the
pioneer in including most of the comforts,
not to say luxuries, which they now take as a
matter of course.

Though the might Ismay brought to the White Star Line
was intimidating, White Star's competitors refused to admit
defeat in the North Atlantic market. In fact, the competition
grew more intense. Cunard was constantly improving its
fleet, and two German companies, North German Lloyd and
the Hamburg-American Line, also became powerful players.
The German companies had a distinct advantage over their
competitors: their government subsidized their shipping
lines. The main reason for this generosity was to ensure that
the ships could be requisitioned in times of war. Although
subsidies might have benefited him financially, Ismay refused
to ask the British government for help with his White Star
Line. He did not want the government involved in his business in any way.

An American Presence

For the most part, America's shipping companies decided
not to enter the North Atlantic competition, ceding maritime superiority to the British and Germans. In the early
1900s, however, the New York banker and steel and railroad
magnate John Pierpont "JP" Morgan decided to enter the
business. A quintessential figure of the Gilded Age, Morgan
was one of the most powerful and richest men in the world.

Like the activities of fellow tycoon Cornelius Vanderbilt, the exploits of JP Morgan often made newspaper headlines. *The New York Times* detailed Morgan's actions at the 1898 launch of *Corsair*, his new 300-foot yacht, as if he were royalty:

> Commodore Morgan was one of the first to get off the train, and he led the way to the platform, which had been erected under the bow of the new yacht. When all the guests had taken their positions Mr. Morgan signaled that all was ready. . . . Commodore Morgan was standing just under the bow, and at his side was [his daughter] Miss Louisa Morgan, with the bottle of wine in her hand, ready to christen the boat. Miss Morgan waited until the yacht had fairly started, and then, swinging the bottle against that bow, said, "I christen thee Corsair." It was one of the prettiest launches ever witnessed. The yacht slid down the ways, gathering speed as she went. She shot out into the river and then a tug . . . brought the new yacht safely alongside the deck.

Four years later, in 1902, Morgan formed the International Mercantile Marine Company and began purchasing many other shipping companies to add to his own. By the end of the year, the International Mercantile Marine Company had finalized a buyout of the powerful White Star Line, then under the leadership of J. Bruce Ismay, who had taken over when his father died in 1899. In the deal, the company

American businessman JP Morgan bought the British White Star Line. It became part of his International Mercantile Marine Company.

allowed Ismay to remain chairman and managing director of White Star; later he was promoted to president of the International Mercantile Marine Company.

As might be expected, the moves Morgan was making were interpreted as threats by many Britons, including the men associated with the venerable Cunard Line. Cunard — with much assistance from a protective British government — responded with a vengeance, commissioning the construction of two ships that would outdo in sheer speed and luxury anything that had been produced by the White Star Line. Those sleek ships, the *Lusitania* and the *Mauritania*, were brought into service in 1907 and immediately became the most talked-about liners on the North Atlantic route.

The gauntlet had been thrown down, and that summer, White Star's Ismay and the president of Harland and Wolff, Lord William James Pirrie, had a meeting to determine how

J. Bruce Ismay, son of the founder of the White Star Line, was president of the International Mercantile Marine Company.

to respond to Cunard's challenge. The idea they came up with would revolutionize the industry. The final plan was to create three superliners that would be among the most luxurious and largest vessels the world had ever seen. To do this, some speed certainly would need to be sacrificed. There would be no Blue Riband coming these ships' way; but as long as they could make the passage in decent and predictable time, White Star did not mind. Besides, the luxury of the voyage would be second to none, and the thought of Gilded Age travelers basking in that luxury left Ismay and Pirrie dreaming of the profits they could make, should superior numbers of travelers choose their ships over others'.

Construction Begins in Ireland

Construction of the first of the three ships, the *Olympic*, began in December 1908 at Harland and Wolff's Belfast shipyard.

The *Titanic*'s construction took place at Harland & Wolff's shipyard in Belfast, Ireland.

Work on the second ship, the *Titanic*, began at the same site the following March. In 1911 construction began on the third ship, originally known as *Gigantic*; its name was changed to *Britannic* after the *Titanic* tragedy. Of the three, the *Titanic* eventually acquired the reputation as the grandest. It also was to become the best known, not only for its untimely and catastrophic demise but also for the grandiosity it represented from the moment it was conceived to the time it left on its maiden voyage on April 10, 1912.

Thanks to Morgan's financial backing, cost was not a great issue in building the *Titanic*. More than three thousand men worked for two straight years to build it. One observer of the ship's construction recorded the spectacle:

[A]t last the skeleton within the scaffolding began to take shape, at the sight of which men held their breaths. It was the shape of a ship, a ship so monstrous and unthinkable that it towered high over the buildings and dwarfed the very mountains by the water. . . . A rudder as big as a giant elm tree, bosses and bearings of propellers the size of a windmill — everything was on a nightmare scale. . . .

An Amazing Spectacle

The roughly 100,000 people who crowded the banks of Belfast's River Lagan on May 31, 1911, to watch the *Titanic*'s launch were treated to a jaw-dropping spectacle. Just short of 883 feet long and 92 feet wide, the steel-constructed steamship weighed more than 46,000 tons. By comparison, Cunard's *Mauritania* and *Lusitania* were 790 feet long, and each weighed less than 32,000 tons. While Cunard's ships could carry 2,200 passengers each, the *Titanic* could hold at least a thousand more. Of course, such luxury came at a price. The total cost to build the *Titanic* was $7.5 million, or roughly $400 million in today's currency. The measures used to keep this cost down would become important issues of debate following its sinking.

The *Titanic*'s hull was divided into sixteen watertight compartments that would be sealed off by doors at a moment's notice. Even if four of the compartments were to become flooded, the ship still could stay afloat. If five compartments were breached, the ship would sink. This, however, was considered an unlikely scenario by *Titanic*'s designers because at that time, there had never been such a severe maritime

On May 31, 1911, the *Titanic* was launched and afloat for the first time. Its engines, boilers, machinery, and fittings were still to be placed.

accident in the North Atlantic. The compartments were formed by fifteen bulkheads, or upright walls. That the bulkheads were not tall enough to reach the top deck would be a major factor in the ship's eventual demise. However, at the time of the *Titanic*'s construction, its designers had reasoned that the ship would never sink low enough to allow water to flow over the tops of the bulkheads and into adjacent compartments.

Though the designers' worst-case scenario is exactly what occurred on April 14, 1912, those viewing the *Titanic*'s launch little more than a year earlier had no reason to mistrust what they had been hearing for months from trade publications and from the White Star Line itself: that the *Titanic* and its sisters were a new breed of ship whose utilization of modern technology had rendered them practically unsinkable. White Star officials later downplayed the fact that the word "unsinkable" had ever been used regarding the *Titanic*. Indeed, even after being informed by several sources

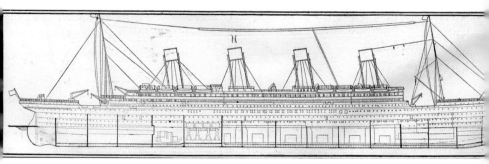

This illustration shows the *Titanic*'s sixteen watertight compartments.

that the *Titanic* had struck an iceberg and was in danger of sinking, White Star's vice president, Phillip Franklin, said "unsinkable" at least twice in speaking with the media:

> There is no danger that *Titanic* will sink.
> The boat is unsinkable, and nothing but
> inconvenience will be suffered by the
> passengers. . . . It is unbelievable that *Titanic*
> could have met with accident without our
> being notified. We had a wireless from her
> late Sunday giving her position, and are
> absolutely satisfied that if she had been in
> collision with an iceberg we should have
> heard from her at once. In any event, the
> ship is unsinkable, and there is absolutely no
> danger to passengers.

Whether Franklin was simply attempting to calm the media frenzy that was swelling by the minute or whether he truly believed that his company's ship was unsinkable cannot

Thomas Andrews, *Titanic's* chief designer, traveled on its maiden voyage. He took copious notes, citing areas that needed refinement and modification.

be known. If there were any people involved in the *Titanic's* construction who believed the ship had safety issues before it set sail on its maiden voyage, none spoke out at a level high enough to result in the documentation of those concerns. It is possible, as well, that any misgivings expressed by a participant in the building of the *Titanic* were overridden by the desire of those further up in the corporate hierarchy, including Ismay and Morgan, to get the *Titanic* and its sister ships out running routes in the North Atlantic. White Star's owners did not want Cunard's new ships to seize too strong a foothold in the luxury market. The chief designer, an Irishman named Thomas Andrews, seemed to have no qualms about the *Titanic*. The nephew of Lord Pirrie, Andrews was on the *Titanic* when the ship he had helped design went down. He had decided to make the voyage so he could take note of any improvements the ship might need.

Following his death, Andrews was cited by the British government for his poor design plans. But as the years wore on, Andrews became universally regarded as a tragic hero, one who stoically went down with the ship he had created.

Two

A Catastrophic Collision

THE MOON WAS NOT VISIBLE in the clear April sky, but passengers could see the stars as the *Titanic* moved across the calm North Atlantic waters on its last night at sea. A growing chill had cleared the ship's decks of people, the formal-wear dinners had ended, and the ship-wide parties that had been a nightly occurrence were winding down as well. All signs pointed to another quiet night at sea for both passengers and crew—until 11:40 p.m., when the lookouts spotted it: a massive iceberg standing directly in the vessel's path. The lookouts immediately rang the warning bell and phoned the bridge.

First Officer William Murdoch was quick to act. He ordered the ship's quartermaster to turn the steering wheel sharply to the left ("hard a-starboard"), then ordered the engines to be reversed ("full stern"), which is similar to putting on the brakes of a car. Murdoch next triggered a switch that closed the watertight doors in the bulkheads below. A head-on collision, which only seconds earlier appeared certain, was avoided. But as the ship passed to the left of the iceberg, chunks of ice broke off and landed on the *Titanic*'s forward well deck, and the starboard side of the hull scraped the iceberg. Over the years, many have suggested that the *Titanic* would have been better off ramming the iceberg head-on, since then the impact would have been absorbed by the stronger bow. Others believe that the correct response would have been to speed up, to allow the *Titanic* to move past the iceberg faster, minimizing the time the berg had to scrape and damage the side of the boat. But Murdoch did not have the benefit of hindsight, nor did he have much time to think things through. So he did what he was trained to do: he swerved and reversed the engines.

Those who were first to become aware of the collision reported various sensations. Frederick Fleet, one of the two lookouts who had first spotted the iceberg, said he heard a "slight grinding noise" and believed the ship had simply skimmed the iceberg, passing by unharmed. Others reported similar stories of grinding sounds, small vibrations, or shudders. Some said it felt as though a propeller had broken off the ship. Many said they felt or heard nothing.

Within minutes, the ship's officers and important representatives of the company were up on the bridge. Included among them were Captain Edward J. Smith, who had been sleeping when the collision occurred, White Star Line director J. Bruce Ismay, and the ship's designer, Thomas Andrews. When the situation was assessed, it turned out to be far worse than the early signs had indicated. The iceberg had punctured the hull below the water's surface, and water was flooding six of the sixteen compartments. One of the earliest detailed reports of damage came from Fourth Officer Joseph Boxhall, who had been ordered to check the front part of the vessel. Boxhall believed the incident to be minor until he was approached by a carpenter who told him otherwise:

Size of the Iceberg

While the exact size of the iceberg the *Titanic* struck is not known, several estimates have surfaced over the years that were based on newspaper reports and eyewitness accounts. Most historians now believe the berg was somewhere in the range of 50 to 100 feet high and 200 to 400 feet long. It is thought that the iceberg rose at least six stories above the waterline. Various photographs have surfaced of bergs that are believed to be the one with which the *Titanic* collided.

Some believe that the *Titanic*'s captain, Edward J. Smith, was pressured to speed through the North Atlantic ice fields that ultimately claimed his ship.

[The carpenter] said, "The ship is making water [leaking]," and he went on the bridge to the captain and I thought I would go down forward again and investigate; and then I met a mail clerk, a man named [John] Smith, and he asked where the captain was. I said, "He is on the bridge." He said, "The mail hold is full" or "filling rapidly" . . . and I proceeded right down into the mail room . . . [T]he water seemed to be then within 2 feet of the deck we were standing on. . . . And bags of mail floating about. I went right on the bridge again and reported to the captain what I had seen."

It did not take long for those in charge of the ship to react to the news that the *Titanic* was sinking. Less than half an hour after the ship struck the iceberg, Captain Smith ordered the uncovering of the lifeboats, then the transmission of a call of distress. Those orders came shortly after midnight on April 15. The distress call was picked up by the Cunard liner *Carpathia*, which was 58 miles away. Its captain, Arthur Rostron, immediately ordered a change of course so that *Carpathia* could assist the sinking *Titanic*.

Stewards rushed from room to room, knocking on doors, waking passengers and directing them to the boat deck, where other crew members helped them put on lifebelts. The loading of the lifeboats was troublesome at best. Though the gallant custom of allowing women and children to board the lifeboats first appeared to be upheld by the crew to the best of its ability, the scene was chaotic, with the result that some panicked men tried — successfully — to circumvent the

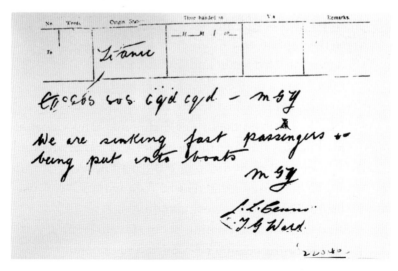

This photograph shows one of the last distress calls placed from the *Titanic*.

Passengers scramble to board one of the few lifeboats on the *Titanic*.

unwritten rule. Others attempting to do so were threatened by gun-carrying crew members. There were tearful scenes as women and children left their husbands and fathers behind when they boarded lifeboats, which were then lowered into the water. Eight-year-old Marjorie "Madge" Collyer was one of those who vividly remembered the scene:

> The decks were full of people. Some of them were crying. An officer said we should all put

The *Californian* Controversy

A much closer British passenger freighter, the *Californian*, also was within range of the distress call, though no one was around to receive it. Earlier that night, the ship's wireless operator, Cyril Evans, had contacted *Titanic* wireless operator Jack Phillips to warn him of ice fields in the area. But when the *Titanic* hit the iceberg, Evans, who was the only operator on the *Californian*, had already gone to bed, leaving the communication device unmanned. The *Californian*'s crew, however, did notice when the *Titanic* began firing a series of rocket flares. Crew members later reported telling their captain, Stanley Lord, what they had seen; but even though the ships were less than 20 miles apart, Lord did not order a change of course. One reason may have been that the firing of rockets was commonplace at the time. Ships used rocket flares for all types of communication at sea. Eventually, at 5:30 on the morning of April 15, the *Californian* began heading in the direction of the *Titanic*. By that time, the *Titanic* already had been under the sea for more than three hours.

on life preservers. . . . Then someone said we should get into a boat and two men lifted me up and put me in a boat. My father raised me in his arms and kissed me, and then he kissed my mother. She followed me into the boat. . . . The stars were shining and it was just like day. Some sailor put a rug around my mother to keep her warm. There were so many in our lifeboat that we had to sit up all the time. Nobody could lie down. My mother was so close to one of the sailors with the oars that sometimes the oar caught in her hair and took big pieces out of it. There was one officer in our boat who had a pistol. Some men jumped into our boat on top of the women and crushed them and the officer said that if they didn't stop he would shoot. Another man jumped and he shot him.

Not Enough Lifeboats for All

Though Madge Collyer's boat was full, other lifeboats that left the *Titanic* were not—especially the ones that left early, before the severity of the situation had been fully recognized. And even if all the lifeboats had been filled to capacity, nearly five hundred people would have been stranded on the sinking vessel. The decision to risk so many lives was made by those who built the ship, who put business and comfort concerns over safety.

At capacity, the ship's twenty lifeboats could carry only 1,178 people, but there were 2,224 passengers and crew on board. These two numbers would become a significant topic

To preserve room and make way for grand designs, lifeboats were kept to a minimum on the *Titanic*. This photo shows passengers strolling past four lifeboats on the upper deck.

of discussion in the days and decades that followed the sinking—as would the significant discrepancies in the relative proportion of passengers saved from each of the ship's classes.

Prior to launching, White Star was well aware that there were not enough lifeboats on the *Titanic* to accommodate all who were aboard, but that was a sacrifice management had chosen to make. Early designs of the ship featured enough davits, or boat lifts, to hold an adequate number of lifeboats. But those extra davits would have taken up much of the room on the first- and second-class promenade decks, an area passengers used to walk around the entire outside of the ship. Much of the ship's lavishness would have been lost if more lifeboats had been added. *Titanic* historian Walter Lord sarcastically summed up the issue in his well-regarded book *The Night Lives On*:

> In the luxury trade, "boats for all" meant less room on the upper decks for the suites, the games and sports, the verandahs and palm courts, and the glass-enclosed observation lounges that lured the wealthy travelers from the competition. On the *Titanic*, for instance, it would sacrifice that vast play area amidships and instead clutter the Boat Deck with (of all things) boats.

Carrying a sufficient number of lifeboats also would have added to the ship's cost and thus eaten away at the owners' profits, specifically by cutting into the number of steerage passengers the *Titanic* could carry. Although steerage tickets were by far the cheapest, the sheer volume of low-income passengers wanting to sail across the Atlantic ensured the shipping companies large amounts of money. Interestingly, although the *Titanic* was designed with the luxury market in mind, it was the steerage passengers who generated the most profit.

Even those who did not believe the ship to be unsinkable at least thought it would stay afloat for many hours, should an accident occur. There would be plenty of time for rescue vessels to arrive on the scene, at which point the lifeboats would serve as little more than ferries moving people from the *Titanic* onto other boats. There were other reasons for not having enough boats for everyone, as well. For example, the route the *Titanic* was traveling was well used and believed to be safe, and planners counted on wireless technology to quickly summon help in the event of an accident. But mostly the owners did not want to sacrifice deck space to lifeboats in the numbers necessary to accommodate everyone aboard the vessel, and they presented as many arguments as possible to convince themselves—and anyone else whose opinion mattered to them—that additional boats were not necessary. Most important, the British Board of Trade required only sixteen lifeboats for a ship over 10,000 tons. The *Titanic* exceeded these criteria and therefore was not in violation of the applicable regulation. However, the Board of Trade's rules were very outdated—they had not been amended since 1894, when the largest ship on the seas was about 13,000 tons. At 46,000 tons, *Titanic* was several times heavier—and consequently able to carry far more people.

The issue of too few lifeboats was not exclusive to the *Titanic*, or to the White Star Line, for that matter. It was rare for any of the larger ships of the day to carry enough lifeboats to accommodate everyone. Some believed that was the wrong approach, including Harland and Wolff's managing director, Alexander Carlisle. Carlisle, like the *Titanic*'s chief designer, Thomas Andrews, also was related (as a brother-in-law) to company president Lord Pirrie. In the earliest stages of the *Titanic*'s construction, Carlisle had suggested that the *Titanic* carry at least forty-eight lifeboats, which would have been sufficient to carry all the passengers and crew, the liner could possibly hold. After the accident, Carlisle told one newspaper he did not agree with the regulations that said the *Titanic* needed only sixteen lifeboats. He said, "As ships grew bigger, I was always in favor of increasing the lifeboat accommodation." In the end, only 706 people were lucky

Two lifeboats make their way to the *Carpathia*.

enough to get spots in the *Titanic*'s lifeboats, eventually to be pulled aboard the *Carpathia* and taken safely to New York.

A Survivor's Story

As those in lifeboats were rowed away from the *Titanic*, water continued to pour into the front of the massive vessel. Survivor Lawrence Beesley later remembered what he witnessed from his lifeboat, which was more than a mile from the wreck when the *Titanic* went down:

> [A]s we gazed awe-struck, she tilted slowly up, revolving apparently about a centre of gravity just astern of amidships, until she attained a vertically upright position; and there she remained — motionless! As she

swung up, her lights . . . went out altogether.
And as they did so [t]here came a noise
which many people, wrongly I think, have
described as an explosion; . . . It was partly
a roar, partly a groan, partly a rattle, and
partly a smash, and it was not a sudden roar
as an explosion would be. . . . [I]t was a noise
no one had heard before, and no one wishes
to hear again: it was stupefying, stupendous,
as it came to us along the water.

At approximately twenty minutes after 2 a.m. on April
15, 1912, the *Titanic* snapped in two between its third and
fourth funnels. The ship's bow half swiftly sank to the bottom of the Atlantic, while the stern portion briefly righted
itself until it had taken on enough water to join its other half
under the surface of the ocean. In the end, 1,518 passengers
and crew were killed. Most of victims died of hypothermia
from being in the frigid 28-degree-Fahrenheit water, though
the official cause at the time was given as drowning. Passengers and crew in ships that passed by the scene recalled dead
bodies scattered about the sea, floating among the *Titanic's*
wreckage. One lady who sailed by on a German passenger
ship, the *Bremen*, later described the heartbreaking scene to
a reporter:

We saw the body of one woman dressed
only in her night dress, clasping a baby to
her breast. Close by was the body of another
woman with her arms clasped tightly round
a shaggy dog. . . . We saw the bodies of

An artist's rendering of the sinking of the *Titanic.*

three men in a group, all clinging to a chair. Floating by just beyond them were the bodies of a dozen men, all wearing lifebelts and clinging desperately together as though in their last struggle for life.

Early Warnings

The ice warnings had begun soon after the *Titanic* entered the North Atlantic waters. On Sunday, April 14, eight of them came across the ship's wireless device, the first coming in the morning from the British liner *Caronia*. It read ". . . bergs, growlers and field ice" had been spotted ahead on the route the *Titanic* was traveling. History has noted that Captain Smith altered the ship's direction later in the evening, likely in response to the multiple warnings; however, he did not reduce the speed at which the ship was traveling. Had the business interests of his employers influenced him to maintain speed even in the face of prospective danger? This question remains unanswered. There is no hard evidence to prove that Captain Smith was pressured to maintain speed. However, owing to stories perpetuated by the media, many people believe that this was the case. There are sound reasons for such an opinion.

The *Titanic* was scheduled to arrive in New York City on Wednesday, April 17. It was imperative for the White Star Line that it do so. After all, the main reason White Star had the ship built was to create a luxurious liner capable of maintaining a schedule its passengers could depend on. Arriving any later than April 17 would damage the *Titanic*'s reputation for reliability before it had had time to establish a good record—thereby jeopardizing White Star's goal of dominating the North Atlantic passenger market. The financial stakes were enormous. The company did not want to disappoint the large crowd of onlookers—not to mention the many members of the press—expected to be waiting in New York Harbor for the *Titanic*'s arrival. The joyous celebration of grandiosity, not to mention the celebratory press coverage the company would receive, would be tarnished by a late arrival. The *Titanic* must arrive no later—or sooner—than April 17.

Over the years, many people have placed the blame for the accident on the belief that White Star had given its employees instructions to keep the ship on schedule at all costs. Based in part on witness testimony, historians have theorized that the company's president, J. Bruce Ismay, put pressure on Captain Smith to maintain a quick pace, even after the icy conditions were clearly known. Ismay consistently denied that charge, saying he had maintained a hands-off position during the emergency and basically had been just another passenger aboard the ship.

The thought that Ismay may have pressured Captain Smith to keep a steady speed was not the only issue that damaged the shipping executive's reputation. Newspaper reports achieved the same effect. And, unlike Captain Smith, who went down with the ship and so died a hero, Ismay jumped into a lifeboat and was later taken aboard the *Carpathia*. For deserting the ship and taking a lifeboat seat that could have gone to someone else, Ismay was labeled a coward, heavily criticized by both the press and the general public for not having adhered to the unwritten rule of saving women and children first. Instead, people believed, Ismay cared only about saving himself. Over the years, historians who have examined these criticisms have noted reports that Ismay helped load women and children into lifeboats, and only when there were no more women or children around did he board a boat.

Ismay's survival allowed him to be questioned about the circumstances leading to the collision. He was also asked to speculate about why the ship did not slow down in response to multiple warnings to the crew that there were icebergs in the vicinity. During the later investigation into the disaster by the U.S. Senate, Ismay said he had left all decisions about whether to slow down or maintain speed in the hands of the ship's crew. In a statement published in the *Times* of London less than two weeks after the *Titanic* sank, Ismay continued proclaiming his innocence:

I hope I need say that [I would not], for
one moment, have thought of getting into
the boat if there had been any women there
to go in it. Nor should I have done so if I
had thought that by remaining on the ship
I could have been of the slightest further
assistance. It is impossible for me to answer
every false statement, rumour, or invention
that has appeared in the newspapers.

Safety Takes a Backseat to Luxury

The world had waited expectantly for its
launching and again for its sailing; had
read accounts of its tremendous size and its
unexampled completeness and luxury; had
felt it a matter of the greatest satisfaction that
such a comfortable, and above all safe boat
had been designed and built—the "unsinkable
lifeboat";—and then in a moment to hear that
it had gone to the bottom as if it had been the
veriest tramp of a steamer of a few hundred
tons; and with it fifteen hundred passengers,
some of them known the world over! The
improbability of such a thing ever happening
was what staggered humanity.

Published just nine weeks after the sinking of the *Titanic*,
the first paragraph of the book *The Loss of the S.S.* Titanic: *Its
Story and Its Lessons* accurately and succinctly describes the
emotional rise and fall the *Titanic* story brought to people

across the world in 1912. The words gained added poignancy because they were written by Lawrence Beesley, one of the lucky seven hundred or so who survived what was then the deadliest accident in maritime history.

Beesley's first-person account of the tragedy begins on the morning of April 10, 1912, with him having breakfast in a hotel in Southampton, England. Sitting behind him, Beesley wrote, were three fellow ticketholders discussing the possibility that the ship they were about to board would become involved in an accident at sea. In the distance, the *Titanic*'s four gigantic funnels could be seen jutting above the Southampton rooftops. It was toward those funnels that Beesley and the unidentified group of travelers headed after they finished eating. They were four of the more than 2,200 people—some 1,320 passengers and nearly 900 crew—who boarded the ship and traveled on its maiden voyage to New York City. A science teacher in England, Beesley was part of the roughly 300 second-class passengers, a group chiefly consisting of middle-class Britons—men, women, and children—traveling on vacation to the United States.

There were two other classes of passengers on the ship, third and first. The majority of the third-class, or steerage, passengers were people from all walks of life from across the world, looking to travel to America in search of opportunities they believed would help improve their lives. The roughly seven hundred steerage passengers on board the *Titanic* were treated nearly as well as first-class passengers had been on older ships. According to Geoffrey Marcus, author of *The Maiden Voyage*, the steerage accommodations on board the *Titanic* compared favorably to first-class quarters on lesser ships:

The *Titanic* leaves the port of Southampton on her maiden voyage, on the morning of April 10, 1912.

[The steerage passengers' rooms] were well ventilated, well heated, and brightly lit by electricity. The third class dining saloon was situated where the vessel's motion was least felt. The third class also had their own smoking-room, general room, and enclosed promenade, provided with chairs and tables, which could be used in any weather. The berths were clean and comfortable. The food was good, if it was plain; and there was plenty of it. All this cost only a few pounds for the trip. It was wonderful value for the money.

While not much has been written about those who traveled second or third class, volumes have been written about those who were among the *Titanic*'s first-class passengers. The wealthiest—if not the most famous—among them was forty-seven-year-old John Jacob Astor IV, who was traveling with his pregnant eighteen-year-old wife, Madeleine Talmage Astor. They were accompanied by his manservant, his wife's maid, a private nurse, and the couple's dog. Astor's magnificent suite included working fireplaces and separate sleeping quarters for the staff. Though he was the richest, Astor was far from the only millionaire traveling on the *Titanic*. Others included industrialist Benjamin Guggenheim, Macy's department store co-owner Isidor Straus and Ida, his wife, and socialite Margaret "Molly" Brown. Although he had a suite specifically built for him, *Titanic* owner JP Morgan was not able to make the trip because he had to attend to other business matters.

The *Titanic*'s three passenger classes were kept strictly apart from each other, and most of the ship's amenities, such as the swimming pool, were reserved for those in first class. Other exclusive first-class features included two barbershops, a gymnasium, multiple libraries, and a forward grand staircase capped by a glass dome. The sheer luxury of the ship's interior would have made it hard for those aboard to suspect any potential structural defects lying below. Not that any passengers would have had reason to anticipate such issues. No ship could go to sea without having passed multiple inspections and without being approved by government officials. Ironically, the grandiosity existed because of sacrifices made in the ship's construction. For example, to allow the ship's passengers easy access to many sections of the vessel that might otherwise be difficult or impossible to get to, the bulkheads could not be constructed perfectly tight.

How Much Did It Cost?

Ticket prices for the *Titanic*'s maiden voyage varied widely, depending on which class the passenger wanted to travel. The most expensive first-class ticket cost more than $4,000 in 1912, or roughly $100,000 in today's dollars. Second-class tickets were $150 (about $3,000 today), and third-class tickets were about $40 (roughly $300 today).

The reading and writing room on Deck A of the *Titanic* was reserved for first-class passengers.

In 1986 *Titanic* historian Walter Lord pointed out several of the ship's safety shortcomings—and the rationale for them—in *The Night Lives On*. Lord compared the *Titanic's* safety features with those of the *Great Eastern,* an English ship launched in the late 1850s that was ultrasafe but not at all passenger friendly:

> [T]he perfect ship was no longer the vessel
> that best expressed the art of the shipbuilder.
> It was the ship that made the most money. . . .
> Passengers demanded attention; stewards
> could serve them more easily if doors were
> cut in the watertight bulkheads. A grand
> staircase required a spacious opening at
> every level, making a watertight deck

impossible. The sweep of a magnificent dining saloon left no room for bulkheads that might spoil the effect. . . . A double hull ate up valuable passenger and cargo space; a double bottom would be enough. . . . One by one the safety precautions that marked the *Great Eastern* were chipped away in the interests of a more competitive ship. . . . When the "unsinkable" *Titanic* was completed in 1912, she matched the *Great Eastern* in only one respect: she, too, had 15 transverse watertight bulkheads. . . . But even this was misleading. The *Great Eastern's* bulkheads were carried 30 feet above the waterline; the *Titanic's*, only 10 feet.

A Near Miss

Many of the first-class passengers boarded the ship in Cherbourg, France, where the *Titanic* had stopped a few hours after its departure from Southampton. As it happened, those passengers avoided the scare the passengers who had boarded in Southampton got shortly after the *Titanic* set out from its berth. That is when the movement of the water displaced by the massive ship broke the thick cables holding the *New York*, a much smaller vessel docked nearby. Had it not been for the intervention of a tugboat, the two larger vessels would have collided. The near miss pointed out the risks inherent in any project, no matter how well planned it is.

The incident caused only a brief delay, but at least one *Titanic* passenger took it as a harbinger of troubles ahead. He reportedly told another passenger, Renee Harris, that he was

This photograph captures the near collision of the *New York* and *Titanic* as the *Titanic* departed from Southampton.

going to get off the ship at Cherbourg. Harris later remembered the conversation she had with that man, who told her, "That was a bad omen. Get off this ship at Cherbourg, if we get that far. That's what I'm going to do." Harris, who would survive the ship's sinking, probably wished she had taken the passenger's advice. Her husband, Henry, a popular theatrical producer in New York City, died when the *Titanic* sank. For most, the incident with the *New York* was a bit unnerving but nowhere near alarming enough to derail their travel plans.

After leaving Cherbourg, the *Titanic* moved through the English Channel and around the southern tip of England to its final precrossing port of call at Queenstown (Cobh), Ireland, where more than one hundred passengers, mostly third class, came aboard. Then it was off to the high seas of the North Atlantic, the market area the ship had been built by the White Star Line to conquer, which would be, instead, the site of its demise.

Three

The Aftermath

THE *CARPATHIA*'S ARRIVAL IN NEW YORK HARBOR at 9:00 p.m. on April 18, 1912, was met by swarms of media professionals and tens of thousands of onlookers. Such a scene, albeit on a smaller scale, was supposed to have happened a day earlier, at the time of the *Titanic*'s scheduled berthing. But by April 18, the *Titanic* had been dominating newspaper pages for three days for another reason, and hardly a soul had not heard what that reason was. Not everything that had been reported was accurate, but the main headline in the April 15 issue of *The New York Times* was "Biggest Liner Plunges to the Bottom at 2:20 a.m." Other outlets took more cautious approaches to their early reporting, and some papers—such as the *Christian Science Monitor* on April 15 ("Passengers Safely Moved and Steamer Titanic Taken in Tow") and the *London Daily Mail* on April 16 ("Titanic Sunk, No Lives Lost")—were just plain wrong. Some of the erroneous information had come directly from the White Star Line, which tried to relay positive information as the facts were being sorted out. It appears that even at this stage, company officials were trying to report the situation in their favor.

When the truth spread to the general public, shock followed closely behind. It was difficult for many to fathom

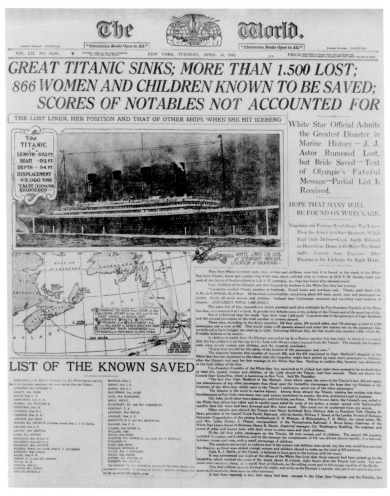

Headlines from New York's April 16, 1912, *The World* announce the sinking of the *Titanic*.

that so many people had died on the widely heralded ship. As the shock faded, people wanted to know why the accident had occurred. Those people included officials of the governments of England and the United States. White Star now would have to defend its practices and address the growing perception that safety had been sacrificed for business reasons.

White Star Leader Questioned

Just one day after the *Titanic* survivors arrived in New York—and the same day as the *Californian's* unheralded arrival in Boston—a U.S. Senate subcommittee led by Senator William A. Smith commenced hearings on the issue with the goal of finding answers and holding accountable for the massive catastrophe any who might be deemed negligent. The first order of business for Smith, a Republican lawyer from Michigan, was to question White Star's managing director, J. Bruce Ismay. Rumor had it that Ismay was planning to quickly disembark the *Carpathia* and make his way back to England before anyone in the United States could question him. Ismay almost instantly had become a scapegoat for the disaster, based on some truths and much innuendo. Along with accusations that Ismay had ordered the captain to continue at a high rate of speed and that he had taken a seat on a lifeboat that could have gone to a passenger, there even were rumors that he had dressed like a woman so the crew would allow him to board. Despite Ismay's denials, the American media and the general public were relentless in attacking him. A letter written by Boston historian Brooke Adams to Francis Newlands, a senator from Nevada, relayed some particularly brutal, yet not uncommon, sentiments:

> Ismay is responsible for the lack of lifeboats,
> he is responsible for the captain who was
> so reckless, for the lack of discipline of the

The U.S. Senate Investigating Committee questions wireless operator Harold Thomas Coffin (seated center) on May 29, 1912, in New York.

crew, and for the sailing directions given to the captain which probably caused his recklessness. In the face of all this he saves himself, leaving fifteen hundred men and women to perish. I know of nothing at once so cowardly and so brutal in recent history. The one thing he could have done was to prove his honesty and his sincerity by giving his life.

Eighty-two witnesses were questioned before the Senate inquiry concluded on May 25. The inquiry yielded more than

1,100 pages of testimony from survivors. In his final report, Senator Smith suggested that many changes were needed in the shipping industry and that many errors had been made by Ismay and the White Star Line regarding the *Titanic*. He concluded that the regulations then used by the British Board of Trade—the organization in charge of setting England's shipping policies—were too lax and should be updated. Specifically, Smith cited the speed of the vessel and the lack of adequate lifeboats, as well as the need for a wireless operator to be on duty every minute of the day. He also singled out Captain Lord of the *Californian*, faulting him for failing to recognize and react in a timely manner to the distress flares of the sinking *Titanic*. Over the years, some historians have criticized Smith's findings, especially since his knowledge of seafaring vessels was limited.

Management Nearly Absolved by British

The British Board of Trade's own inquiry was well under way by the time the U.S. Senate committee wrapped up its investigation. The British hearings had begun on May 2 and were headed by John Charles Bigham, a High Court judge more commonly known as Lord Mersey. The hearings lasted eight weeks, during which time ninety-six witnesses were called to testify, including Captain Lord of the *Californian*, who again was interrogated about why he had not responded to the *Titanic*'s distress signals. In his final report, issued on July 30, Lord Mersey wrote:

> [T]he truth of the matter is plain. . . . The rockets sent up from the *Titanic* were distress signals. The *Californian* saw distress signals.

The British Board of Trade

Established in the seventeenth century, the British Board of Trade was an advisory committee intended to promote trade and increase revenue from Britain's colonial possessions, in particular the American colonies. Crucial to the *Titanic* case, the board also set safety standards for ocean liners, and a board representative had signed off on the *Titanic* before its maiden voyage. Today, most of the agency's functions have been taken over by other branches of the British government.

The number sent up by the *Titanic* was
about eight. The *Californian* saw eight. . . .
It was suggested that the rockets seen by
the *Californian* were from some other ship,
not the *Titanic*. But no other ship to fit this
theory has ever been heard of. . . . When she
first saw the rockets the *Californian* could
have pushed through the ice to the open
water without any serious risk and so have
come to the assistance of the *Titanic*. Had she
done so she might have saved many if not all
of the lives that were lost.

Lord Mersey's findings essentially absolved Captain
Smith and the White Star Line of blame for the disaster.
The company's business practices were hardly questioned.
Instead, Lord Mersey attributed the main causes of the accident to the icy conditions and placed most of the blame for
the massive loss of life on the inaction of the *Californian*'s
captain. Lord Mersey's report recommended that changes
be made to regulations regarding the design of ships' watertight compartments and that boat crews receive improved
training. He also suggested that wireless stations on passenger ships be manned around the clock. Lord Mersey did
suggest that, in the future, each ship carry enough lifeboats
for everyone on board, but he did not blame the loss of life
on White Star for not having adequately supplied the *Titanic*.

Continuing Public Scrutiny

The prevailing thought was that the inquiries conducted
by the U.S. and British governments had provided enough

Recovering the Bodies

The cable steamer *Mackay-Bennett* arrived on the scene of the *Titanic* accident on April 20, the day after the U.S. Senate hearings had begun. White Star had contracted the ship almost immediately after the *Titanic* sank, charging its crew with the dreadful task of recovering as many bodies as possible. The ship came from Halifax, Nova Scotia, carrying more than one hundred wooden coffins, embalming equipment, and tons of ice to help keep the bodies preserved as well as possible for the return trip to Halifax, where undertakers waited. The scene was more horrific than most had expected. Bodies were scattered everywhere, supported by the lifebelts passengers and crew had donned to help save themselves. As each body was plucked from the frigid Atlantic waters, crew members gave it a number, documented any details they could, and made note of any personal belongings. Some of the information gathered was fairly detailed and later helped people identify the bodies of loved ones. Other information was cryptic and of little help at all.

The *Mackay-Bennett* recovered fifty-one bodies on its first day at work, but almost half were in such poor shape that they had to be buried at sea. The steamer left the scene on April 26, having recovered 306 bodies, 116 of which were buried at sea. Three other ships were sent after the *Mackay-Bennett* had arrived. Of the 328 bodies that were found, 209 were brought back to Halifax. There, 59 were identified by friends and relatives and transported to various places for burial. Some 150 bodies were buried in Halifax, at one of three cemeteries: Mount Olivet, Baron de Hirsch, or Fairview Lawn. Almost 1,200 bodies were never found.

answers to prevent legal challenges. This did not prove to be the case, however, and criticism of the White Star Line continued. As clergymen delivered their first post-tragedy sermons, many did not attempt to hide their strong personal feelings about the incident. In many instances, the perceived "me-first" mentality of the White Star Line and the elite of the Gilded Age bore the brunt of the attacks from pulpits. Reverend Dunbar Ogden of Atlanta, Georgia, said, "It is easy to condemn when a great ship goes down, but is not our nation living, as the *Titanic* traveled that fateful night, in absolute disregard of human life?" Dr. Charles Parkhurst was even harsher as he spoke to the congregation at Madison Square Presbyterian Church in New York City. He believed the fault lay with the company, which focused on the all-mighty dollar at the expense of the safety of its passengers:

> The picture which presents itself before my eyes is that of the glassy, glaring eyes of the victims, staring meaninglessly at the gilded furnishings of this sunken palace of the sea; dead helplessness wrapt in priceless luxury . . . . Everything for existence, nothing for life. Grand men, charming women, beautiful babies, all becoming horrible in the midst of the glittering splendor of a $10,000,000 casket! . . . The two sore spots which . . . constitute the disease that is gnawing into our civilization are love of money and passion for luxury. Those two combined are what sunk the *Titanic* and sent 1,500 souls prematurely to their final account.

Disaster Becomes Desperation

The impact due to the loss of so many lives was vast and stretched worldwide, but nowhere was it more directly felt than in the homes of those who had perished. Many aboard the ship had been primary breadwinners, and their deaths left huge financial, as well as emotional, holes. Much of the grief was centered in Southampton, England, the place the majority of the *Titanic*'s crew members had called home. News that the *Titanic* had gone down hit the port city extremely hard. Years later, one Southampton native recalled his childhood memories of the disaster:

> People were running round the street
> "the *Titanic* sunk" panic, panic stations
> everywhere. Women running out and
> going down to the Shipping Office, you
> know, down near the dock gates there and
> the *Titanic*, they can't sink the *Titanic* because
> everybody talked about the *Titanic*, it was
> the unsinkable ship . . . there wasn't a family
> in the whole area that never had anybody
> associated with that ship. Fathers and sons
> on board, grandsons and all this sort of
> thing. . . ."

Southampton's mayor explained to one reporter exactly how desperate the situation was in his city. He said some six hundred families, with an average size of five people each, had been left with no means of support and had to be cared for by someone. "For more than a month," he said, "most of these families . . . had been kept alive by the mayor's fund

Anxious crowds gather outside the White Star Line's office, awaiting news of the *Titanic*'s survivors.

[charity] . . . and many of them have sold or pawned everything that could raise money. Now, even where husbands are safe, they have lost all their clothes and not infrequently the money they possessed."

The pride so many Southamptoners had felt because their sons had played a role in the building and sailing of the greatest piece of machinery man had ever built was gone. In its place were desperation, misery, and pain.

Four

Seasons of
Change

THE ENORMITY OF THE EVENT all but guaranteed the *Titanic* tragedy a place in history. But exactly what, if any, specific impact the disaster would have on the world at large, and the shipping industry in particular, was anybody's guess. It did not take long for answers to emerge.

The first major incident came less than ten days after the *Titanic* had sunk. On April 24, 1912, fifty-four crew members from *Titanic*'s sister ship *Olympic* went on strike as the vessel was about to leave Southampton, bound for New York. The workers refused to set sail because the ship did not have enough lifeboats for everyone on board, and the trip was canceled. The workers were all arrested on charges of mutiny, though those charges later were dismissed, and most of the men returned to the ship. It was a small gesture, but it was only the first of many to come.

The first major change to maritime policy stemmed from the inquiries conducted by the U.S. and British governments in the immediate aftermath of the accident. In the United States, the inquiry and subsequent final report resulted in the passage of Senate Bill Number 6976, also known as the Smith Bill, which codified some of the recommendations presented by Senator William Smith. Those recommendations, based on Smith's committee hearings, included the following:

> Prior to departure, passengers must be assigned to lifeboats, of which there will be enough for all;
> Every ocean steamship with one hundred or more passengers must carry two electric searchlights;
> There must be a radio operator on duty at all times;
> The firing of rockets or candles on the high seas for any reason other than as a signal of distress would be a misdemeanor;
> Upgrades must be made to the quality of ships' hulls and also to each ship's bulkheads.

The British inquiry also resulted in the implementation of a number of regulations intended to make sea travel safer, most notably the stipulation that every ship carry enough lifeboats to hold everyone on board.

The plight of the *Titanic* turned the spotlight on an issue that had been gaining momentum for several decades: the safety of life at sea. Throughout the ages, people had simply assumed that those who traveled and worked on the high seas did so knowing of the risks involved and accepting the situation. For the most part, shipping companies were left to run their businesses as they wished, with little regulation from government. The regulations that were in place mostly were there to satisfy insurance companies, which would have to reimburse policyholders whose ships were lost or damaged. Therefore, the insurance companies wanted to make sure the ships they covered met certain criteria. But the safety of those sailing the ships was of little concern. Almost immediately after the *Titanic* went down, much of that changed.

Radio Waves

The lack of an on-duty radio operator aboard the *Californian*—which many believed would have helped save the lives of hundreds of those who died when the *Titanic* went down—spurred the passage of a major U.S. law. It was called the Radio Act, and it was signed into law by President William Howard Taft in the summer of 1912. The act called for a ship's wireless equipment to be monitored at all times (echoing a recommendation of the Senate report released a few months earlier), required radios to have a range of at least 100 miles, and stated that all wireless operators must be licensed. The last stipulation helped free the airwaves of traffic from thousands of amateurs who were using personal wireless devices at the time.

On November 12, 1913, the first International Convention on the Safety of Life at Sea (SOLAS) began in London. Created in direct response to the *Titanic* disaster, the conference lasted until early 1914, and seventy-four new regulations governing conduct in international waters were agreed upon by the thirteen participating countries. The new covenants included rules regarding the number of lifeboats, continuous radio monitoring, and more. The meeting also established an international ice patrol, to be charged with cruising the shipping passages of the North Atlantic looking for icebergs

During the summer of 1912, President William H. Taft signed into law the Radio Act, which called for all ships' radios to be manned at all times. This is a photograph of the *Titanic*'s radio room.

that might pose a danger and warning ships accordingly. As important as the specific changes agreed upon at the SOLAS convention were, the body had another significant effect, as well. This was the recognition by major maritime countries of the importance of working together on setting international shipping regulations, rather than relying on individual countries to set — or sometimes *not* set — their own laws.

International Ice Patrol

When the *Titanic* sank in April 1912, there was no official body keeping track of dangerous icebergs in the North Atlantic. Ships making the crossing had to rely solely on their own lookouts, and cruising at night, when visibility was low, was very dangerous. The International Ice Patrol was formed to help address those problems. Because the United States had the most direct experience patrolling the area, the task of finding and issuing warnings about icebergs was assigned to the U.S. Coast Guard, with the expenses shared among thirteen nations with interests in the North Atlantic shipping routes.

The following year, 1915, the U.S. Congress passed the Seamen's Act, which helped improve sailors' working conditions. Prior to the act, most sailors worked long hours for little pay, which meant the quality of workers that ship owners could attract generally was low. But the Seamen's Act, implemented as a direct result of the *Titanic* disaster, changed that. It mandated better living and working conditions for those sailing on ships weighing more than 100 tons, except for vessels that operated in rivers. Specifically, the act regulated the number of hours a sailor could work, did away with corporal punishment for disobedience or desertion, and established minimum standards for cleanliness and safety. The prospect of working on the high seas suddenly became a bit less threatening.

For some people, however, nearly immediate changes to the laws were not enough to compensate for the distress they believed the *Titanic* disaster had caused them, so they chose to sue. Eighteen-year-old survivor Thomas Whiteley, a saloon steward from Manchester, England, was one such litigant. Whiteley's first brush with fame had come a few days after the sinking of the *Titanic*, when he allowed a newspaper reporter to interview him from his hospital bed in New York City. In the resulting story, Whiteley claimed to have heard the *Titanic*'s lookouts talking about how they had given three warnings of icebergs ahead to those in control of the ship prior to the fatal collision, and all three warnings had been ignored. As the end approached, the newspaper story read, Whiteley was thrown from the sinking ship and swam to a nearby lifeboat, which is where he met the lookouts and heard their story. Whiteley reported that one of the men said "that at a quarter after eleven o'clock on Sunday night, about twenty-five minutes before the great ship struck the berg, that he had told First Officer Murdock [sic] that he believed he had seen an iceberg." He goes on to say,

> He said he was not certain, but that he saw the outline of something which he thought must be a berg. A short time later, the lookout said, he noticed what he thought was another mountain of ice. Again, he called the attention of the first officer to it. A third time he saw something in the moonlight which he felt certain was an iceberg. The air was cool and there were indications in his mind that there were bergs in the neighborhood. A third time he reported to the first officer that he had seen an iceberg. This time, as I recall it, he did not say merely that he fancied he saw one, but that he had actually seen one. His words to the officer, as I remember them, were—"I saw the iceberg. It was very large, and to me it looked black, or rather a dark gray instead of white."

After his release from the hospital, Whiteley returned to his home in England. He was not heard from until nearly two years later, when the *Times* of London reported that Whiteley had sued the Oceanic Steam Navigation Company, White Star's parent company, for negligence in regard to the *Titanic* disaster. A court date was set, but no records have been found stating what happened next, leading some historians to speculate that the parties settled out of court.

The Thomas Ryan Lawsuit

One of the best-known *Titanic*-related lawsuits was filed by a retired Irish farmer named Thomas Ryan. The elderly Ryan was the father of twenty-nine-year-old Patrick Ryan, a passenger aboard the *Titanic* who was killed when the ship went down. Thomas Ryan claimed that his son's death had left him destitute because Patrick, a cattle farmer, had been the older man's sole means of support. The suit alleged that negligence on the part of the Oceanic Steam Navigation Company executives was to blame. Ryan's attorney claimed that the ship:

> was operating at an excessive speed given the conditions, which included darkness, ice and haze;
> failed to have enough lifeboats in relation to the number of people on board;
> failed to provide proper lookout and to furnish on-duty lookouts with binoculars, and;
> failed to provide adequate training for the crew on the operation of the lifeboats that were available.

The suit was heard on June 20, 1913, by a London jury, which sided with Ryan and awarded him $500, plus court costs. The decision opened the door for many others to file lawsuits of their own, which they began doing in droves both in England and the United States. By 1916 more than $18 million worth of claims had been filed in the United States alone. Eventually, a settlement in the amount of $665,000 was reached between the Oceanic Steam Navigation Company and all the U.S. plaintiffs. The small settlement came out to roughly $430 for every person who died in the disaster. Terms of the settlement also stated that the company could never again be sued for *Titanic*-related damages.

The accident itself—if not the threat of lawsuits in addition to those already pending—spurred White Star and other companies to implement immediate, self-imposed changes to their fleets long before legislation would require such measures. For example, the *Olympic* was removed from service and retrofitted by Harland and Wolff with a supply of lifeboats that was more than adequate. Its bulkheads also were raised to a level that could withstand flooding, and a second layer of steel was added by extending the double bottom up the sides of the ship's hull. Suddenly, features that had been deemed prohibitively expensive by the ships' owners became both affordable and a priority.

Similar design changes were made to White Star's *Britannic*, which was being constructed at the time the *Titanic* went down. However, even the new design elements—which included the addition of a double steel hull and more lifeboats—could not save the *Britannic* from its ultimate fate. This sister of the *Titanic*, requisitioned as a hospital ship by the Royal Navy during World War I, struck a mine laid in the Aegean Sea by a German submarine. On November 21, 1916, the mine blew a large hole in the vessel's right side, and the *Britannic* began flooding. The captain ordered the ship evacuated and lifeboats lowered. More than one thousand people were on board, but only thirty died, even though the ship itself ended up on the bottom of the Kea Channel. In fact, with the new and improved bulkheads adding extra weight, the *Britannic* sank faster than the *Titanic*.

Titanic survivor Violet Jessop also survived the sinking of the *Britannic*, on which she was working as a nurse. In her memoirs, Jessop, who had been floating in a lifeboat before she was rescued by a motorboat, described the gruesome scene of her second brush with maritime disaster:

> The first thing my smarting eyes beheld
> was a head near me, a head split open, like
> a sheep's head served by the butcher, the
> poor brains trickling over on to the khaki
> shoulders. All around were heartbreaking
> scenes of agony, poor limbs wrenched out
> as if some giant had torn them in his rage.
> The dead floated by so peacefully now, men
> coming up only to go down again for the last
> time, a look of frightful horror on their faces.
> Wreckage of every sort was everywhere
> and, at a distance, stricken *Britannic* slowly
> ploughed her way ahead . . . she dipped
> her head a little, then a little lower and still
> lower. . . . Then she took a fearful plunge,
> her stern rearing hundreds of feet into the air
> until with a final roar she disappeared into
> the depths.

For a while at least, fate was much kinder to the *Olympic*, the third of the three luxury superliners White Star had built for the North Atlantic market. *Olympic* also was requisitioned by the British during World War I but survived the deadly conflict and returned to public service. The ship came to be known as "Old Reliable"—until May 15, 1934, that is. On that day, as the *Olympic* was making its way into New York Harbor in dense fog, it crashed into the lightship Nantucket, slicing the stationary vessel in two and killing seven of its eleven crewmen. The *Olympic* was scrapped the following year.

New Safety Organizations Are Born

The issue of maritime safety the *Titanic* disaster had made so prominent soon was forced to take a backseat to the Great Depression and World Wars I and II. But at the end of World War II, in 1945, the United Nations (UN) once again took up the cause. In 1948 the UN created an agency called the Inter-Governmental Maritime Consultative Organization (IMCO) to help govern the shipping industry. Many of the improvements in ship safety that soon would be made resulted from experience gleaned during World War II.

The IMCO, which held its first meeting in 1959, earned a reputation as a "rich man's club" because it was controlled by the wealthy countries of the Northern Hemisphere and was not at all representative of everyone in the world. The agency changed its name to the International Maritime Organization (IMO) in 1982 and today has 169 member states, including the United States and the United Kingdom, the two countries primarily associated with the *Titanic*. The IMO focuses on ships' technical aspects and has many sub-committees that consider topics such as ship design, maritime safety, radio communication, fire protection, and pollution. The agency then proposes legislation in these categories but cannot enforce it. That is left to the individual countries. This often is an area of concern, according to the IMO:

The problem is that some countries lack
the expertise, experience and resources
necessary to do this properly. Others perhaps
put enforcement fairly low down their list of
priorities. . . . IMO has plenty of teeth but
some of them don't bite. The result is that
serious casualty rates—probably the best
way of seeing how effective governments
are at implementing legislation—vary
enormously from flag to flag [from country
to country]. The worst fleets have casualty
rates that are a hundred times worse than
those of the best. . . . The most important
IMO conventions contain provisions for
Governments to inspect foreign ships that
visit their ports to ensure that they meet
IMO standards. If they do not they can be
detained until repairs are carried out.

Classification societies are another piece of the ship
safety puzzle. The societies help establish technical standards for ships. Those include minimum standards for hulls,
engines, steering, and other vital parts. There are more than
fifty classification societies worldwide. During the *Titanic's*
day, the number was far lower, and the societies' current governing body, the International Association of Classification
Societies (IACS), which was formed in 1968, did not exist.

Five

Long-Term Impacts

Suddenly, without warning . . . a Philippine tanker carrying 8,800 [barrels] of petroleum products collided with the *Doña Paz* [on December 21, 1987]. Immediately, the tanker's cargo ignited, setting the sea aflame. As the inferno engulfed both ships, dozens of passengers leaped, diving deep to avoid the burning waters. Swimming beyond the fiery oil, Eugenio Orot, 27, surfaced hundreds of feet away from the ferry. As the anguished screams of children calling "Nanay!" (mother) and "Tatay!" (father) echoed around him, he searched desperately for his two children and wife, but to no avail. Within four hours, the *Doña Paz* and the [tanker] were gone.

TIME MAGAZINE'S DETAILED ACCOUNT of the collision between the 2,215-ton Philippine passenger ferry *Doña Paz* and the 629-ton oil tanker *Vector* hardly does justice to the enormity of the catastrophe. The accident was so brutal that finding

Bodies of the victims of the *Doña Paz* disaster in 1987 are laid out in the Philippines.

any words to quantify it would be difficult. In the end, the collision in the shark-infested Tablas Strait killed more than 4,500 people. The ships themselves were so badly damaged that they sank to the bottom of the sea in just a few hours. The death toll rendered the incident the deadliest peacetime maritime disaster in world history, a dubious title once held by the *Titanic*.

Only twenty-six people survived the *Doña Paz* disaster, most of them by diving beneath the water to escape the flaming surface of the sea. Thirty-four-year-old fisherman Pampilo Culalia was standing on the ferry's deck when the collision occurred. He said he saw his father-in-law jump into the water and quickly followed suit, leaving behind his brother, his fourteen-year-old daughter, and his ten-year-old niece. After swimming some distance, Culalia turned around to look at the wreckage. He later said, "I saw the ship in flames and I wanted to kill myself. But God shook me and woke me."

Safety reports issued after the accident were harrowing:

> The *Doña Paz* was carrying nearly three times the number of passengers it was licensed to hold.
> At the time of the accident, some of the ship's officers reportedly were watching television or drinking beer instead of manning their posts.
> Lifejackets were stored inside lockers that were locked.
> Eight hours had passed before Philippine maritime authorities learned of the accident (it appears that neither vessel sent out distress signals), and another eight hours went by before search and rescue operations were organized.
> The oil tanker *Vector* was operating with an expired license, did not have a proper lookout in place, and was running without a qualified master.

Several other major maritime disasters have occurred since the *Titanic* sank on April 15, 1912. Some came during wartime, notably the sinking of the German ship *Wilhelm Gustloff* in the Baltic Sea by the Soviet Union toward the end of World War II. More than eight thousand civilians and soldiers were killed, making the sinking the world's greatest maritime disaster ever. War also took down Cunard Line's once-revered *Lusitania*, which was torpedoed in 1915 by a German submarine off the coast of Ireland. The ship sank in 18 minutes, killing 1,119 passengers and crew.

New Regulations Established

Incidents such as those that killed thousands in the twentieth century proved that unsafe sailing conditions were not a thing of the past. Public awareness of the poor safety measures put in place by the *Titanic*'s builders had led to many changes, but there still were numerous problems due to the lack of systematic regulations. One of the main issues plaguing sea travel over the years has been the existence of variances in the governing rules and conventions. Because ships commonly travel lengthy distances across the globe, they are subject to many different sets of rules and regulations. Factors such as which country a ship is from, which port it is stopping at, and which country its owners are from all come into play. In the *Titanic*'s time, and still today, difficulties were common.

But there is little doubt that overall, life on the high seas is much safer now than it was during the *Titanic*'s day, owing in large part to the regulations established in response to the disaster of 1912. The *Andrea Doria*, for instance, was a ship that clearly benefited from such changes. While traveling west across the North Atlantic on the night of July 25, 1956, the Italian liner collided in a heavy fog with the *Stockholm*, a much smaller Swedish ship that was heading east out of New York Harbor. The *Stockholm* rammed the starboard side of the *Andrea Doria*, ripping it open and allowing access

The *Andrea Doria* sinks off the coast of Nantucket after its collision with the *Stockholm* in 1956.

to the raging waters of the sea. The Italian liner sank eleven hours later, but not before all but 46 of the 1,706 passengers and crew were rescued. Those who were killed died because of injuries suffered at the time of the collision. The high survival rate has been attributed to the improved radio communication brought about by the *Titanic* tragedy, which made possible rapid responses by nearby ships. But, in the case of the *Andrea Doria*, even the best safety devices—which included modern radar—proved incapable of preventing the collision. Harry Manning, captain of the luxury liner *United States*, perhaps best explained why. Speaking about the *Andrea Doria* disaster, Manning said, "Despite all the safety gadgets, the mind is supreme and the mind is fallible."

Human fallibility played an important role not only in the *Titanic* tragedy but also in subsequent investigations that searched for the physical cause of the liner's demise. For years, most people believed the iceberg had ripped a gash

Robert Ballard, finder of the *Titanic* wreck, speaks at a conference in 2003. At his left is a projection of the wreckage.

in the side of the ship's hull, which led to the eventual sinking of the vessel. But evidence uncovered decades later with the help of modern technology showed that this likely was not the case. For more than seventy years, adventurers had searched the bottom of the sea for the *Titanic*'s wreckage, but it was not until the summer of 1985 that it was found by a team of French and American researchers. The ship was nearly 2.5 miles underwater. The team was led by American Robert Ballard, who gave an emotional press conference following the discovery:

The *Titanic* lies in 13,000 feet of water on
a gently sloping alpine-like countryside
overlooking a small canyon below. Its bow
faces north and the ship sits upright on the
bottom. Its mighty stacks point upward.
There is no light at this great depth and little
life can be found. It is a quiet and peaceful
place and fitting place for the remains of
this greatest of sea tragedies to rest. It may
forever remain that way and may God bless
these now-found souls.

Despite Ballard's wishes that others leave the *Titanic*
alone, his discovery was followed by more exploration of the
sunken vessel. In the years to come, crews from other expeditions salvaged what they could from the ship's remains,
including jewelry, money, and other artifacts. No bodies,
however, will ever be found.

The scavenging expeditions stirred up many emotions
among people, including Ballard, who believed that the
Titanic wreckage essentially was a large gravesite that should
never be disturbed. But visits to the ship did help shed new
light on the exact reason the *Titanic* went down. Sonar
scans of the bow—which was buried under some 45 feet of
mud—revealed that the ship had not been lost because of a
300-foot-long gash in the hull, as originally believed. Rather,
Titanic sank because of a series of six small slits made by
the iceberg along the first six of the ship's sixteen compartments. Each slit was no wider than 3 inches, and the longest
was 30 feet. In addition, the force of the collision itself broke
the heads off the rivets that connected the hull's steel plates.

Treasures from Beneath the Sea

Since the site of the *Titanic* wreck was discovered in 1985, a number of expeditions to the area have been mounted, and more than six thousand items have been recovered and put on display. Most are in museums, some have been returned to the descendants of people lost on the ship, and a small proportion has, controversially, been sold to collectors. Items retrieved from *Titanic* include the following:

The ship's bell and steam whistles.
China dishes and silver utensils from the ship's dining halls.
Dozens of vials of perfume.

Brass window frames, skylights, and deck signs.
Women's brushes, combs, and hairpins.
Unopened wine bottles.
Bars of soap, still wrapped and preserved by the cold.

In August 1998 a large piece of the *Titanic*'s hull was recovered.

The theory is that so many tons of water entered the ship so quickly because the plates, no longer riveted together, split open and allowed free access.

In the late 1990s, a large section of the hull was hoisted to shore, and the metal of the rivets was tested for strength. It was found to be weaker than it have should been, mostly because of a high sulfur content. Most of the steel used in shipbuilding in the early 1900s contained sulfur, but the amount in *Titanic*'s steel was significantly greater than the norm. In fact, all the metal used in the hull was subsequently tested and found to have characteristics that caused it to become brittle under cold-water conditions. This evidence added more fuel to some people's long-standing speculation that the builders of the *Titanic* used cheap, poor-quality materials to keep construction costs as low — and their profits as high — as possible.

Six

A Titanic Legacy

For the sinking of the *Titanic* was the first scene in the last act of a drama that had slowly unfolded for centuries. The same energies that powered the [Gilded] Age would, like a flywheel spinning too fast, soon tear it apart. When the waters of the North Atlantic closed over the *Titanic*'s stern that cold April night, something changed in the Western world, though no one knew it at the moment. Attitudes, beliefs, and values that had endured for hundreds of years were shaken, overnight as it were, and would remain unsettled more than eighty years later.

FOR MANY—INCLUDING DANIEL ALLEN BUTLER, who wrote the quoted passage in 1998—the loss of the *Titanic* and all that the magnificent ship symbolized marked the beginning of the end of the Gilded Age. The era's excess, the nearly unlimited wealth and grandiosity, the arrogant belief that man and his technology could conquer nature, began fading from existence twenty minutes before midnight on April 14,

1912, when the man-made liner met nature's gigantic floating wall of ice. More evidence that the Gilded Age might be
finished came during the first days following the *Titanic* tragedy, when newspapers began to highlight the death numbers
for each passenger class.

The statistics certainly were upsetting. Sixty-two percent
of the 324 first-class passengers on board the ship survived.
Forty-one percent of the 277 second-class passengers survived. Yet of the 706 third-class passengers, only 25 percent
of the people in steerage made it off the ship and into the
lifeboats. Broken down further, the discrepancies between
classes are even more startling, especially where women and
children are concerned:

> In first class, 32 percent of the men, 97
> percent of the women, and all of the children
> survived.
> In second class, 8 percent of the men, 86
> percent of the women, and all of the children
> survived.
> In third class, 16 percent of the men, 46
> percent of the women, and 34 percent of the
> children survived.

Needless to say, the public was outraged by the discrepancies, and claims were rampant that classism had played a
great role in determining who was seated in the insufficiently
numerous lifeboats. Even during his official inquiry, Senator
William Smith dedicated great lengths of time to the subject.
When asked by a reporter why he felt the need to make this
effort, which included extra time spent interviewing survivors, Smith answered passionately:

Second-class passengers board the *Titanic* at its last stop, in Queenstown, Ireland.

The horrible impression remains on my mind that the people of the steerage did not get half a chance. [A survivor] testified to having seen in the last minutes a crowd of men and women from the steerage appear on the upper decks. Why hadn't those steerage people appeared on the deck before? Had they been restrained from doing so?

The Role of Classism in the Disaster

At the time of Smith's inquiry, rumors were circulating that there had been a locked gate separating the steerage section and the upper deck of the ship, where the lifeboats were located. One passenger Smith interviewed confirmed those rumors. Irishman Daniel Buckley said, "They tried to keep us down at first on our steerage deck. They did not want us to go up to the first-class place at all. . . . There was one steerage passenger there, and he was getting up the steps, and just as he was going in a little gate, a sailor came along and chucked him down . . . into the steerage place." Buckley went on to add that the gate he mentioned had not originally been locked, but the sailor had locked it after observing the passenger attempting to leave the steerage area. Other witnesses interviewed by Smith testified that they never saw any locked barrier that would have stopped them from gaining access to the boat deck.

Whether or not a locked gate or door impeded the escape of third-class passengers, the ship's design most assuredly had. Steerage passengers were housed in the lower decks of the boat and, unlike travelers in other classes, they had no direct access to the boat deck. Officials offered other reasons for the low survival rates of third-class passengers, including language barriers and a lack of available stewards to notify them that anything out of the ordinary had occurred. Some even hypothesized that third-class passengers inherently believed themselves inferior to the other passengers and therefore somehow *deserved* to be the ones who died.

Following his country's inquiry, England's Lord Mersey came to the conclusion that the third-class passengers had not been discriminated against in any way. He believed they had not been treated unfairly and offered his own thinking on why a far greater percentage of those passengers had perished than members of any other class:

> It has been suggested before the Enquiry that the third-class passengers had been unfairly treated; that their access to the boat deck had been impeded; and that when at last they reached that deck the first- and second-class passengers were given precedence in getting places in the boats. There appears to have been no truth in these suggestions. It is no doubt true that the proportion of third-class passengers saved falls far short of the proportion of the first and second class, but this is accounted for by the greater reluctance of the third-class passengers to leave the ship, by their unwillingness to part with their baggage, by the difficulty in getting them up from their quarters, which were at the extreme ends of the ship, and by other similar causes.

Those who did not believe the first-class passengers had been favored often pointed to the list of prominent people who had gone down with the ship. That unhappy list includes the richest person on board, John Jacob Astor, and such notables as Benjamin Guggenheim, Isidor and Ida Straus, Captain Smith, and the ship's builder, Thomas Andrews. If classism had played any role in who had perished in the disaster, would not those people have been among the first placed onto lifeboats at the expense of any and all others? And what about the first-class men who, survivors recalled, had assisted from the deck as women and children of all classes departed on lifeboat after lifeboat? Why were they not leaving instead of helping?

Although the *Titanic* disaster had a huge impact on the Gilded Age, it strangely did little long-term harm to the reputation of the company responsible for creating such grandiosity. White Star suffered at first, but after parting ways with the much-despised—at least by those in the United States—J. Bruce Ismay, the company regrouped and temporarily resumed its spot as one of the world's top freight and passenger lines. Ironically, it was rival Cunard that eventually swallowed the White Star name following a merger in the mid–1930s.

A Story That Never Dies

Greed still motivates many business decisions one hundred years after the *Titanic* disaster highlighted the dangers inherent in possessing such a self-serving belief system. When large-scale disasters take place today—such as what is now considered to be the world's worst accidental oil spill following the explosion of the Deepwater Horizon rig in the Gulf of Mexico from April through July 2010—they frequently are attributed to companies that sought to maximize profits at the expense of safety. Other times, they are the result of

This is one of the last photographs taken of the *Titanic* as it left the port of Queenstown, Ireland. It would sink four days later.

lax regulations. Too frequently, it is a little of both. On a positive note, such disasters often are catalysts for wholesale changes in a particular industry, as was the *Titanic*'s sinking to the shipping industry.

For its part, the *Titanic* story has become legendary. The mystery and romance the *Titanic* inspired during its day have been shared with younger generations through books, films, and song, one of the most popular of which still maintains its spot as a campfire song in summer camps across the United States. It is simply titled "The *Titanic*."

> O they built the ship *Titanic* to sail the ocean
>   blue
> And they thought they had a ship
> that the water would never go through.

But the Lord's almighty hand
Knew that ship would never land
Oh she was far from England
And approaching to the shore,
When the rich refused to associate with the
    poor
So they put them down below
Where they were first to go

As the humble closed their eyes
in the darkness of the hold,
The rich upstairs were playing cards for gold
And they laughed when a sailor said,
"There's an iceberg close ahead."

When the Captain heard the news
From a sailor up the mast,
He said, "Steady boys, we'd better not go too
    fast."
But the company in their greed
Said, "We must increase the speed."

Oh they put the lifeboats out
O'er the raging stormy sea,
And the band on board played "Nearer My
    God to Thee"
Little children wept and cried
As the waves swept o'er the side.

[chorus]
It was sad when that great ship went down.

It was sad (it was sad) It was sad (mighty sad).
It was sad when that great ship went down.
Husbands and wives, little children lost their lives.
It was sad when that great ship went down.

Children chant the song, clapping their hands and bellowing the chorus in unison. The irony of the happy demeanor they exhibit while singing about one of the greatest tragedies in world history fails to register. On April 15, 1912, men, women, and children lost their lives. And although it may have been sad when that great ship went down, the changes brought about by the accident, most would agree, are to be celebrated. In many aspects of life today, safety still is sacrificed for business interests. But that does not mean the *Titanic*'s legacy did not give the world reason to sing.

Timeline

1867   Thomas Ismay acquires the White Star Line.

1869   Ismay creates the Oceanic Steam Navigation Company; construction begins on White Star's *Olympic* at the Harland and Wolff shipyard in Belfast, Ireland.

1891   Joseph Bruce Ismay becomes a partner alongside his father at Ismay and Imrie.

1899   The death of Thomas Ismay leaves his son, J. Bruce, in charge of the White Star Line.

April 1907   J. Bruce Ismay and Lord James Pirrie meet to plan construction of three massive luxury liners.

March 1909   *Titanic's* keel is laid at Harland and Wolff.

May 31, 1911   *Titanic* is officially launched.

April 10, 1912   *Titanic* leaves Southampton, England, and sets sail on its first voyage, nearly colliding with liner *New York*.

April 14, 1912, 11:40 p.m.   Less than a minute after lookout Frederick Fleet calls a warning, *Titanic*, cruising at a speed of more than 20 knots, strikes an iceberg in the North Atlantic.

April 14, 1912, 11:50 p.m.   Ten minutes later, an inspection by ship's crew reveals several feet of water in the ship's forward compartments.

April 15, 1912, midnight   Captain Edward Smith is told that the *Titanic* will not remain afloat for long. He orders the first wireless call for distress.

April 15, 1912, 12:05 a.m.   The first orders to abandon ship are given, and lifeboats are ordered uncovered. There are not enough lifeboats for everyone on board.

April 15, 1912, 12:15 a.m.   *Titanic* fires its first rocket flare.

April 15, 1912, 12:25 a.m.   Less than 60 miles away, SS *Carpathia* acknowledges *Titanic's* rocket firing and heads toward the doomed liner.

April 15, 1912, 1:40 a.m.   *Titanic's* last rocket flare is fired.

April 15, 1912, 2:15 a.m.   The last lifeboat is lowered.

April 15, 1912, 2:20 a.m.   *Titanic's* stern rises out of the water and breaks apart from the bow, which promptly sinks. After righting itself for a few moments, the stern takes on too much water and also sinks.

April 15, 1912, 4:10 a.m.   *Carpathia* arrives on the scene and begins pulling survivors from the frigid waters of the North Atlantic.

April 17, 1912   The *Mackay-Bennett* departs from Halifax, Nova Scotia, to search for bodies. Other ships later join in the search. A total of 328 bodies are recovered, 209 of which are brought back to Halifax. The rest are buried at sea.

April 19, 1912   U.S. Senate hearing on the *Titanic* disaster begins. More than eighty witnesses are called over the course of the investigation, which ends on May 25.

May 2, 1912   British Board of Trade inquiry begins. It ends on July 3, with more than ninety witnesses having testified.

1913   International Ice Patrol is created as a direct result of the *Titanic* tragedy.

1914   *Titanic*'s sister ship *Britannic* is launched. The ship will sink two years later, during World War I.

1935   *Titanic*'s sister ship *Olympic* is scrapped after more than two decades of service.

1985   The wreck of the *Titanic* is discovered in two pieces 2.5 miles below the surface in the North Atlantic.

1997   The blockbuster film *Titanic* is released worldwide. The movie wins eleven Academy Awards and becomes the highest-grossing film of all time, a record that stands for more than a decade.

2009   Last survivor of the *Titanic*, Millvina Davis, dies at age ninety-seven.

Notes

Chapter One

p. 9, "Sinking? Of course the *Titanic* couldn't be sinking . . .": Violet Jessop, *Titanic Survivor* (Dobbs Ferry, NY: Sheridan House, 1997), pp. 126–127.

p. 16, ". . . more like an imperial yacht . . .": Daniel Allen Butler, *"Unsinkable": The Full Story* (Mechanicsburg, PA: Stackpole Books, 1998), p. 5.

p. 17, "I consider that he . . .": Sir Bertram Hayes, quoted by Donald Hyslop, Alastair Forsyth, and Sheila Jemima: *Titanic Voices: Memories from the Fateful Voyage* (New York: St. Martin's Press, 1998), p. 10.

p. 18, "Commodore Morgan was one of the first . . .": "Launching of the Corsair," *The New York Times*, December 13, 1898, http://query.nytimes.com/mem/archive-free/pdf?_r=1&res=9E00E4D61438E433A25750C1A9649D94699 ED7CF (accessed May 1, 2010).

p. 22, "[A]t last the skeleton within the scaffolding . . .": Wyn Craig Wade, *The Titanic: End of a Dream* (New York: Rawson, Wade Publishers, 1979), p. 11.

p. 24, "There is no danger that *Titanic* will sink . . .": Phillip Franklin, quoted in Tom Kuntz, ed., *The Titanic Disaster Hearings: The Official Transcripts of the 1912 Senate Investigation* (New York: Pocket Books, 1998), pp. 468–469.

Chapter Two

p. 27, "Frederick Fleet, one of the two lookouts . . .": quoted in Tom Kuntz, ed., *The Titanic Disaster Hearings*, p. 183.

p. 29, "[The carpenter] said, 'The ship is making water,'":

quoted in Tom Kuntz, ed., *The Titanic Disaster Hearings*, p. 136.

p. 31, "The decks were full of people . . .": quoted in Judith P. Geller, *Titanic: Women and Children First* (New York: W. W. Norton, 1998), p. 119.

p. 36, "In the luxury trade, 'boats for all' meant less room . . .": Walter Lord, *The Night Lives On* (New York: William Morrow & Co., 1986), p. 85.

p. 37, "As ships grew . . .": quoted in Lord, *The Night Lives On*, p. 88.

p. 38, "As we gazed . . .": Lawrence Beesley, *The Loss of the S.S. Titanic: Its Story and Its Lessons* (Boston: Houghton Mifflin, 1912), pp. 115–116.

p. 39, "We saw the body . . .": quoted in Butler, *"Unsinkable": The Full Story*, p. 200.

p. 40, ". . . bergs, growlers . . .": quoted in Stephanie Barczewski, *Titanic: A Night Remembered* (London: Hambledon and London, 2004), p. 10.

p. 43, "I hope I need say that . . .": quoted in Paul Louden-Brown, "Ismay and the Titanic" (excerpted from The White Star Line: An Illustrated History 1869–1934), The *Titanic* Historical Society, www.titanic1.org/articles/ismay.asp (accessed on May 10, 2010).

p. 43, "The world had waited expectantly for its launching . . .": Beesley, *The Loss of the S.S.* Titanic, pp. 1–2.

p. 45, "[Their rooms] were well ventilated, well heated . . .": Geoffrey Marcus, *The Maiden Voyage* (New York: The Viking Press, 1969), p. 38.

p. 48, "[T]he perfect ship was no longer the vessel . . .": Lord, *The Night Lives On*, pp. 31–32.

p. 50, "That was a bad omen. Get off this ship . . .": quoted in Barczewski, *Titanic: A Night Remembered*, p. 4.

Chapter Three

p. 51, "Biggest Liner . . .": quoted in Willard Grosvenor Bleyer, *Newspaper Writing and Editing* (Boston: Houghton Mifflin, 1913), p. 12.

p. 51, "Other outlets took more cautious approaches . . .": "Inaccurate Reporting," The Library of Virginia, www.lva.virginia.gov/exhibits/titanic/titbad.htm (accessed May 2, 2010).

p. 53, "Ismay is responsible for the lack of lifeboats": quoted in Butler, *"Unsinkable": The Full Story*, p. 182.

p. 55, "The truth of the matter is plain . . .": *British Wreck Commissioner's Inquiry Report*, 1912, www.titanicinquiry.org/BOTInq/BOTReport/BOTRepCalifornian.php (accessed on May 11, 2010).

p. 60, "It is easy . . .": quoted in Wade, *The Titanic: End of a Dream*, p. 65.

p. 60 "The picture which . . ." : Wade, *The Titanic: End of a Dream*, pp. 65–66.

p. 61, "People were running round the street . . .": quoted in Barczewski, *Titanic: A Night Remembered*, p. 267.

p. 62, "For more than . . .": quoted in Barczewski, *Titanic: A Night Remembered*, p. 270.

Chapter Four

p. 69, "He said he . . .": "Lookouts' warnings of icebergs thrice disregarded within half hour of crash declares steward," *The New York Herald*, April 21, 1914, A-1, www.encyclo pedia-titanica.org/white-star-whiteley.html (accessed on May 11, 2010).

p. 70, "By 1916, claims filed in the United States . . .": "End Titanic Suits By Paying $665,000," *The New York Times*, July 29, 1916, p. 9.

p. 72, "The first thing . . .": Jessop, *Titanic Survivor*, p. 177.

p. 74, "The problem is . . .": International Maritime Organization, "Frequently Asked Questions" and "Flag State Implementation," www.imo.org/about/pages/FAQS.aspx and www.imo.org/OurWork/Safety/Implementation/Pages/flagstateimplementation.aspx (accessed on May 12, 2010).

Chapter Five

p. 75, "Suddenly, without warning . . . a Philippine tanker . . .": Howard Chua-Eoan and Nelly Sindayen, "The Philippines Off Mindoro, a Night to Remember: A Ferry and a Tanker Collide in Titanic Disaster," *Time*, January 4, 1988, 51.

p. 77, "I saw the ship . . .": quoted in Sheila S. Coronel, "Searchers Find No Trace of 1,500 from 2 Ships Sunk in Philippines," *The New York Times*, December 22, 1987, www.nytimes.com/1987/12/22/world/searchers-find-no-trace-of-1500-from-2-ships-sunk-in-philippines.html

?sec=&spon=&partner=permalink&exprod=permalink (accessed on May 2, 2010).

p. 79, "Despite all the . . .": quoted in Kevin F. McMurry, *Deep Descent: Adventure and Death Diving the Andrea Doria* (New York: Touchstone, 2001), p. 35.

p. 81, "The *Titanic* lies in 13,000 feet of water . . .": Doug Cumming, "Discoverers of *Titanic* Return Triumphantly to Woods Hole," *Providence Journal*, September 10, 1985, A1.

Chapter Six

p. 85, "For the sinking of the *Titanic* was the first scene . . .": Butler, *"Unsinkable": The Full Story*, pp. 221–222.

p. 87, "The horrible impression remains . . .": quoted in Wade, *The Titanic: End of a Dream*, p. 254.

p. 88, "They tried to keep . . . : quoted in Wade, *The Titanic: End of a Dream*, p. 254.

p. 89, "It has been suggested before the Enquiry . . .": *British Wreck Commissioners Inquiry Report*, www.titanic inquiry.org/BOTInq/BOTReport/BOTRep3rdClass. php (accessed on May 2, 2010).

p. 92, "O they built . . .": Author unknown, "The *Titanic*," *Encyclopedia Titanica*, www.encyclopedia-titanica.org/ titanic_folk.html (accessed on April 3, 2010).

Further Information

Books

Adams, Simon. *Titanic*. New York: DK Publishing, 2009.

Ballard, Robert D. *Titanic: The Last Great Images*. Philadelphia: Running Press, 2008.

Morrow, Ann. *The Gilded Age*. New York: Children's Press, 2007.

Vander Hook, Sue. *The Titanic*. Edina, MN: ABDO Publishing, 2008.

DVDs

Secrets of the Titanic, National Geographic, 1999.

Titanic: The Complete Story, A&E Home Video, 2002.

Websites

Encyclopedia Titanica
www.encyclopedia-titanica.org
This site contains many thorough articles on the history of the *Titanic* and an excellent alphabetic list of all the ship's passengers, including details about their lives, which lifeboat, if any, they were seated on, their age, and the class in which they had traveled.

RMS Titanic, Inc.

www.titanic-online.com

This site features news updates on *Titanic*-related events as well as comprehensive information on the ship's features, ship-related expeditions and exhibitions, and more.

The Titanic Historical Society

www.titanichistoricalsociety.org

The Titanic Historical Society, established in 1963, is the world's largest *Titanic* organization.

Bibliography

Books

Barczewski, Stephanie. *Titanic: A Night Remembered*. London: Hambledon and London, 2004.

Beesley, Lawrence. *The Loss of the S.S. Titanic: Its Story and Its Lessons*. Boston: Houghton Mifflin, 1912.

Bleyer, Willard Grosvenor. *Newspaper Writing and Editing*. Boston: Houghton Mifflin, 1913.

Butler, Daniel Allen. *"Unsinkable": The Full Story*. Mechanicsburg, PA: Stackpole Books, 1998.

Geller, Judith P. *Titanic: Women and Children First*. New York: W. W. Norton, 1998.

Hyslop, Donald, Alastair Forsyth, and Sheila Jemima: *Titanic Voices: Memories from the Fateful Voyage*. New York: St. Martin's Press, 1998.

Jessop, Violet. *Titanic Survivor*. Dobbs Ferry, NY: Sheridan House, 1997.

Kuntz, Tom, ed. *The Titanic Disaster Hearings: The Official Transcripts of the 1912 Senate Investigation*. New York: Pocket Books, 1998.

Lord, Walter. *A Night to Remember*. New York: Bantam Books, 1955.

———. *The Night Lives On*. New York: William Morrow & Co., 1986.

Marcus, Geoffrey. *The Maiden Voyage*. New York: Viking Press, 1969.

Matsen, Brad. *Titanic's Last Secrets*. New York: Hachette Book Group, 2008.

McMurry, Kevin. *Deep Descent: Adventure and Death Diving the Andrea Doria*. New York, Touchstone, 2001.

Wade, Wyn Craig. *The Titanic: End of a Dream*. New York: Rawson, Wade Publishers, 1979.

Websites

British Wreck Commissioners Inquiry Report. www.titanicinquiry.org/BOTInq/BOTReport/BOTRep3rdClass.php

Encyclopedia Titanica—"The Wreck of the Titanic"—www.encyclopedia-titanica.org/titanic_folk.html

The New York Times Online Archives—December 13, 1898. query.nytimes.com/mem/archive-free/pdf?_r=1&res=9E00E4D61438E433A25750C1A9649D94699ED7CF

The Library of Virginia—"Inaccurate Reporting." www.lva.
virginia.gov/exhibits/titanic/titbad.htm

The New York Times Online Archives, December 22, 1987.
www.nytimes.com/1987/12/22/world/searchers-find-no-
trace-of-1500-from-2-ships-sunk-in-philippines.html?sec=&
spon=&partner=permalink&exprod=permalink

The Titanic Historical Society—"Ismay and the Titanic."
www.titanic1.org/articles/ismay.asp

Index

Page numbers in **boldface** are illustrations.

About the Author

JEFF BURLINGAME is the author of roughly twenty books, including *Prisons* and *Government Entitlements* for Marshall Cavendish Benchmark's series Controversy! In 2007 the New York Public Library named one of his books to its annual Books for the Teen Age list. Burlingame also has been a writer and an editor for various newspapers and magazines and has won more than a dozen awards in that capacity. He has been interviewed on camera as a featured author on A&E's respected *Biography* TV series and has taught and lectured at various writing workshops and libraries across the Pacific Northwest. He resides with his family in Washington State.